S-Factor Prayer Journal

Unless otherwise indicated, all Bible references are taken from the New King James Version®. Copyright©1982 by Thomas Nelson. Used by permission. All rights reserved. Scripture quotations from The Authorized (King James) Version. Rights in the Authorized Version in the United Kingdom are vested in the Crown. Reproduced by permission of the Crown's patentee, Cambridge University Press.

Book cover designed by **Raman Bhardwaj** (front cover) and **Bridgette Bastien** (back cover)

Interior page elements designed by **Bridgette Bastien**

Special thanks to **Vivienne Morana** for assistance with the journal concepts

S-Factor Prayer Journal

Copyright ©2020 Bridgette Bastien. All rights reserved. This book or any portion thereof may not be reproduced or used in any manner whatsoever without the express written permission of the author or publisher except for the use of brief quotations in a book review.

ISBN-13: 978-1-7328798-4-3

ISBN-10: 1-7328798-4-2

S-Factor Prayer Journal

Prayer SAVED My Life
A SERIES BY **Bridgette Bastien**

S-Factor Prayer Journal

SALVATION IS A FREE GIFT, UNWRAP IT!

Salvation is the most important factor in life. We may know this, but living in a busy and complicated world makes it very challenging to prioritize our spiritual lives. Like so many of us, you may want to build a stronger relationship with God and have been searching for ways to get closer to Him. Search no further!

The S-Factor Prayer Journal is just what you need at this stage and phase of your life. It complements S-Factor—the second book within the Prayer Saved My Life Series. It's a great resource to help strengthen your faith in God as you consistently connect with your Heavenly Father. This prayer journal was inspired and strategically designed to ensure you'll have open, honest, and engaging encounters with God.

There are several ways to maximize your prayer journaling experience. First, it's highly recommended that you **read the related chapters in the book, S-Factor,** before you begin journaling. Second, whenever you feel most comfortable, you should share what you've learned with someone else. We grow spiritually when we bless others. Third, don't forget to enjoy the process.

The S-Factor Prayer Journal is divided into three sections:

Prayer – Communicate with God like you would a friend. Choose whether to write out your prayer requests and/or express what's on your mind through pictures and drawings.

S-Factor Prayer Journal

Saved – Meditate on key Bible verses relating to each chapter's topic and insights from S-Factor that resonates with you. Record relevant scriptures and your "Aha" moments. They will be instrumental when you transition to the soul-searching part of the journaling process.

My Life – Invest time in self-reflection based on the questions in each section and the Bible verses you've highlighted in S-Factor. You'll have the opportunity to ask God some critical questions, document His response (based on His divine timing), evaluate your spiritual growth, as well as commit to influencing those in your life.

During the journaling process, you'll experience a deeper intimacy with God. He begs us, "Come now, and let us reason together" (Isaiah 1:18) because He wants us to know Him personally. You'll get a better understanding of your heart's desires. We are urged in Lamentations 3:40 to "Test and examine our ways, and return to the Lord!" Your past, present, and future will have more meaning in light of God's plan.

Although this journey will primarily be about your relationship with God, it's also important to sow good seeds into the lives of others. The Bible says "Iron sharpens iron, and one man sharpens another" (Proverbs 27:17). This means we should build genuine relationships, reflect Christ's character, and help those we can, to reach their full spiritual potential.

My prayer is that while you read S-Factor and pour out your soul onto these pages, you'll proclaim, *'Prayer Saved My Life.'* I also pray that you'll develop a longing for God's presence, a desire to study the Bible more, and a willingness to help others accept God's gift of salvation.

Let the Journey Begin!

S-Factor Prayer Journal

*"This will be written for the generation to come,
That a people yet to be created may praise the Lord."*
Psalm 102:18

S-Factor Prayer Journal

Table of Contents

S-Factor 1: Suicidal 1

S-Factor 2: Setbacks and Setups 6

S-Factor 3: Silent Sufferers 11

S-Factor 4: Stolen by Sleep 16

S-Factor 5: Sorrow in the Soul 21

S-Factor 6: Secrets and Schemes 26

S-Factor 7: Seventy times Seven 31

S-Factor 8: Speck of Sawdust 36

S-Factor 9: Seeing the Spirit 41

S-Factor 10: Speak, Savior 46

S-Factor 11: Seeking Sinners 51

S-Factor 12: Sincerely Saved 56

S-Factor 13: Salvation in Sychar 61

S-Factor 14: Simply ? 66

Closing Thoughts: Salvation Is 71

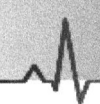
S-Factor Prayer Journal

S-Factor Prayer Journal

PRAYER

> Have you or someone you know struggled with suicidal thoughts or attempted suicide? Pray for deliverance and spiritual breakthrough.

S-Factor Prayer Journal

**If you prefer, you can express your PRAYER
in a picture or drawing.**

S-Factor Prayer Journal

SAVED

Based on this chapter, what scriptures or insights from S-FACTOR have inspired you to draw closer to God and experience His saving grace?

"The thief does not come except to steal, and to kill, and to destroy. I have come that they may have life, and that they may have it more abundantly."
John 10:10

S-Factor Prayer Journal

MY LIFE

After self-reflection, what questions do you have? What are you thankful for? How will you make a difference in someone's life?

QUESTIONS FOR GOD
DATE ASKED:

ANSWERS FROM GOD
DATE RECEIVED:

I'M **THANKFUL** FOR

I'LL TAKE THESE ACTIONS **TO HELP OTHERS**

#SFactorPrayerJournal #PSML

S-Factor Prayer Journal

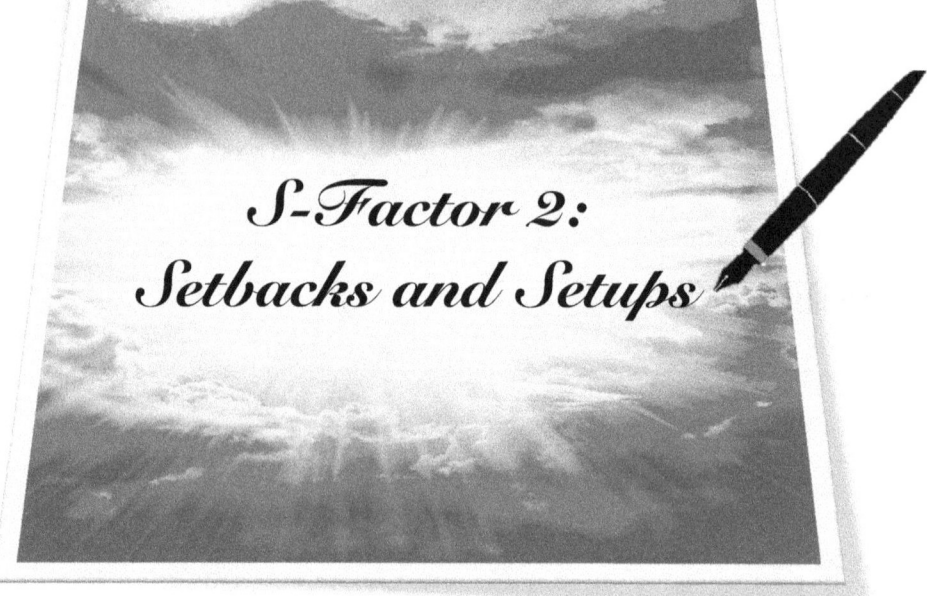

S-Factor 2: Setbacks and Setups

S-Factor Prayer Journal

PRAYER

> What setbacks (trials) have you gone through or are you experiencing now in your life? What setups (blessings) are you earnestly praying for?

S-Factor Prayer Journal

If you prefer, you can express your PRAYER in a picture or drawing.

SAVED

Based on this chapter, what scriptures or insights from S-FACTOR have given you a better perspective of your setbacks and setups?

"And we know that all things work together for good to those who love God, to those who are the called according to His purpose."
Romans 8:28

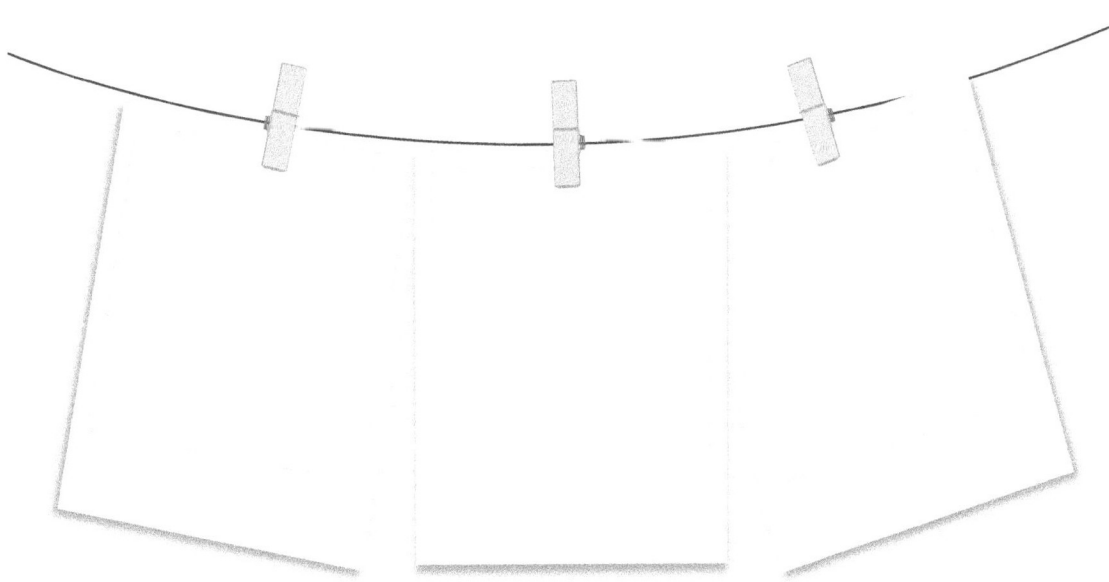

S-Factor Prayer Journal

MY LIFE

Each setback and setup has a purpose. What questions do you have? What lessons have you learned? Who will you encourage?

QUESTIONS FOR GOD
DATE ASKED:

ANSWERS FROM GOD
DATE RECEIVED:

I'VE **LEARNED** THESE LESSONS

I'LL **ENCOURAGE SOMEONE** DEALING WITH SETBACKS

#SFactorPrayerJournal   #PSML

S-Factor Prayer Journal

S-Factor Prayer Journal

PRAYER

Suffering in silence or keeping secrets? Do you feel like there's no one you can trust without being judged? If so, pray and trust in God.

S-Factor Prayer Journal

**If you prefer, you can express your PRAYER
in a picture or drawing.**

S-Factor Prayer Journal

SAVED

Based on this chapter, what scriptures or insights from S-FACTOR give you strength to persevere and hope despite your struggles?

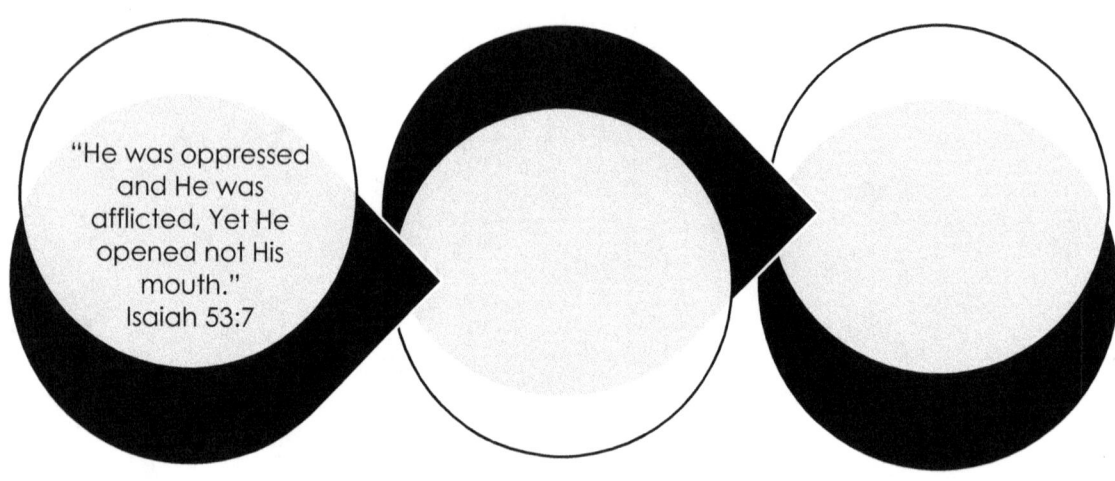

"He was oppressed and He was afflicted, Yet He opened not His mouth."
Isaiah 53:7

#SFactorPrayerJournal　　　#PSML

S-Factor Prayer Journal

MY LIFE

> Running away from God because of pain? DON'T! Reason with Him, sing His praises, then as He leads you, speak up for yourself and others.

QUESTIONS FOR GOD
DATE ASKED:

ANSWERS FROM GOD
DATE RECEIVED:

I'M **PRAISING** GOD FOR

I'LL **SPEAK UP** FOR THOSE WITHOUT A VOICE

#SFactorPrayerJournal   #PSML

S-Factor Prayer Journal

PRAYER

> Losing a loved one can be a traumatic life experience. If you or someone you know is mourning, pray for peace and comfort.

S-Factor Prayer Journal

If you prefer, you can express your PRAYER in a picture or drawing.

SAVED

Based on this chapter, what scriptures or insights from S-FACTOR uplift your spirit when you remember those you have loved and lost?

"Jesus said to her, 'I am the resurrection and the life. He who believes in Me, though he may die, he shall live.'"
John 11:25

S-Factor Prayer Journal

MY LIFE

Death is inevitable. What questions do you have? How do you deal with grief? How can you support those who are mourning?

QUESTIONS FOR GOD
DATE ASKED:

ANSWERS FROM GOD
DATE RECEIVED:

I **DEAL WITH GRIEF** BY

I CAN **OFFER THIS** TO THE BEREAVED

#SFactorPrayerJournal #PSML

S-Factor Prayer Journal

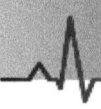

S-Factor Prayer Journal

PRAYER

> Have you been interceding for your child(ren)? Keep praying. God hears your heart's desires even when you can't put them into words.

S-Factor Prayer Journal

**If you prefer, you can express your PRAYER
in a picture or drawing.**

SAVED

Based on this chapter, what scriptures or insights from S-FACTOR remind you that God cares about children and will do anything to save them?

"The Lord is near to the brokenhearted and saves those who are crushed in spirit."
Psalm 34:18

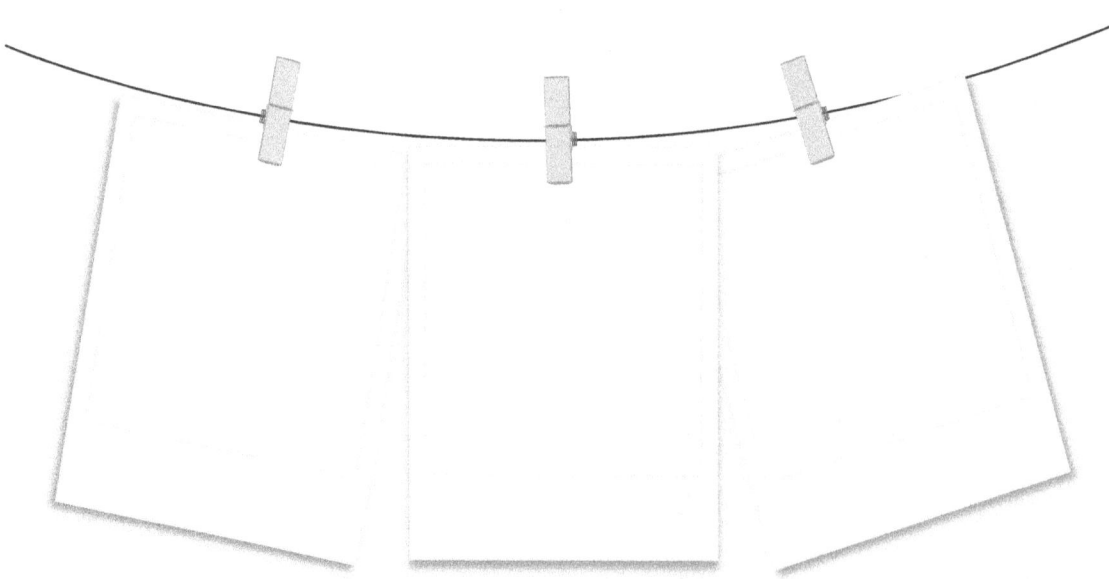

S-Factor Prayer Journal

MY LIFE

Sorrow and sickness are realities. What questions do you have? Do you know any kids who are suffering? How can you brighten their day?

QUESTIONS FOR GOD
DATE ASKED:

ANSWERS FROM GOD
DATE RECEIVED:

PRAYING FOR KIDS WITH THESE ILLNESSES

I'LL **INVEST MORE** IN THIS CHILD'S GROWTH

#SFactorPrayerJournal   #PSML

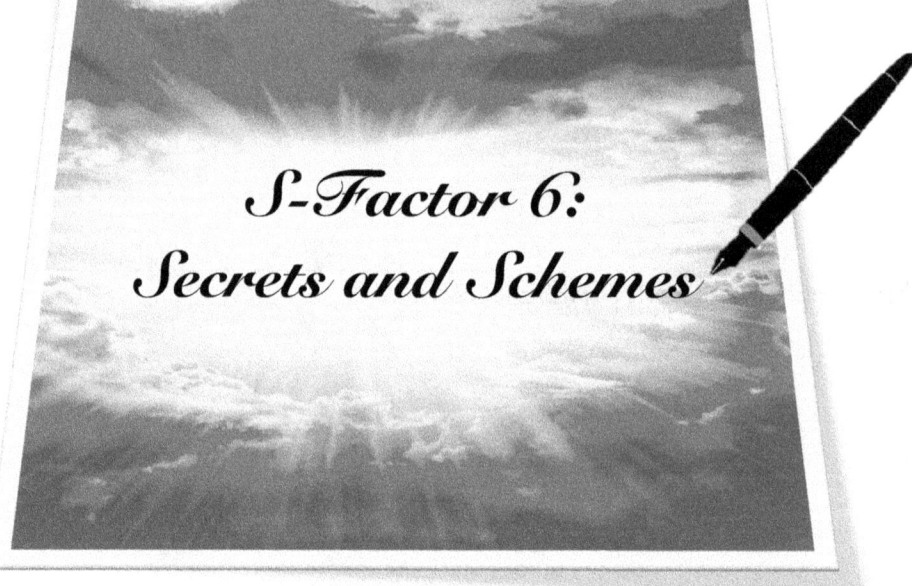

S-Factor Prayer Journal

PRAYER

Have you ever devised a deceptive plan or scheme to get ahead, to get revenge, or to restore your honor? Pray! God is willing to forgive.

S-Factor Prayer Journal

**If you prefer, you can express your PRAYER
in a picture or drawing.**

SAVED

Based on this chapter, what scriptures or insights from S-FACTOR deter you from plotting against someone or keeping secrets that violate trust?

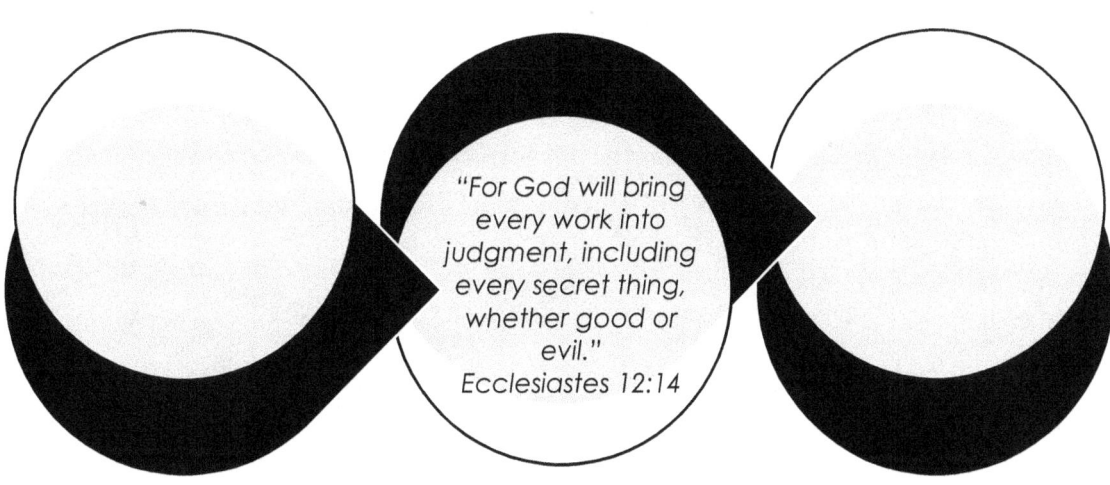

"For God will bring every work into judgment, including every secret thing, whether good or evil."
Ecclesiastes 12:14

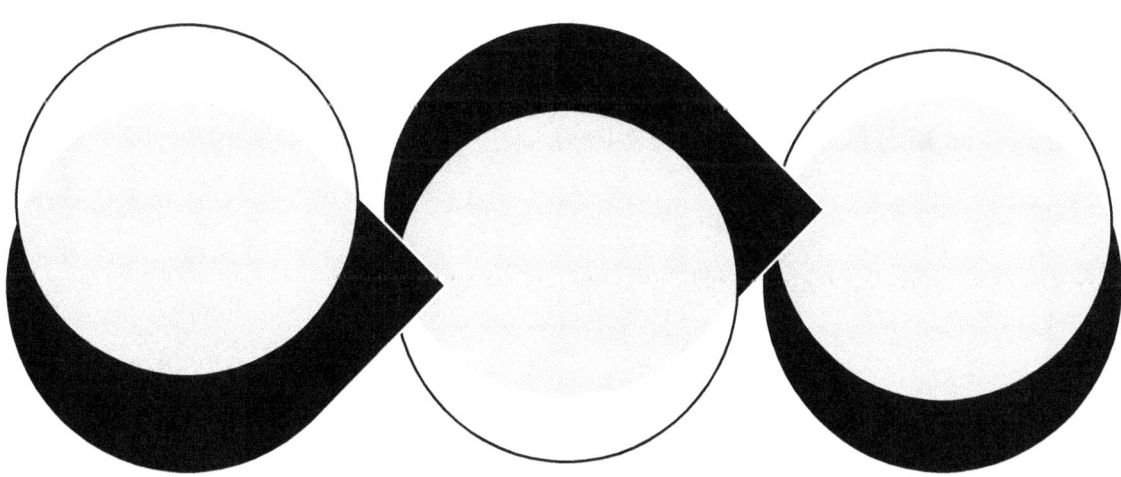

S-Factor Prayer Journal

MY LIFE

God hates deception. Do you wear an invisible mask to fit in? Are you willing to remove it and encourage others to reflect Christ's character?

QUESTIONS FOR GOD
DATE ASKED:

ANSWERS FROM GOD
DATE RECEIVED:

I'LL NO LONGER WEAR THESE **INVISIBLE MASKS**

I'LL **BETTER REFLECT** JESUS WHEN I'M…

#SFactorPrayerJournal　　　　　#PSML

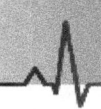

PRAYER

Are you in a relationship with unforgiveness? Pray for a compassionate and loving heart that doesn't want to remain angry or keep malice.

S-Factor Prayer Journal

**If you prefer, you can express your PRAYER
in a picture or drawing.**

SAVED

Based on this chapter, what scriptures or insights from S-FACTOR have given you a new perspective on the importance of forgiving others?

"Love suffers long and is kind; love does not envy; love does not parade itself, is not puffed up; does not behave rudely, does not seek its own, is not provoked, thinks no evil."
1 Corinthians 13:4-5

S-Factor Prayer Journal

MY LIFE

> God says forgive 70 times 7. What questions do you have? Did you forgive yourself for past mistakes? Who else should you forgive?

QUESTIONS FOR GOD
DATE ASKED:

ANSWERS FROM GOD
DATE RECEIVED:

I **FORGIVE MYSELF** FOR

I WILL **FORGIVE** _____ AND **APOLOGIZE** TO _____

#SFactorPrayerJournal #PSML

S-Factor Prayer Journal

PRAYER

What insecurities have kept you from reaching your goals or embracing love? Pray that you'll begin to see yourself through Heaven's eyes.

S-Factor Prayer Journal

**If you prefer, you can express your PRAYER
in a picture or drawing.**

S-Factor Prayer Journal

SAVED

Based on this chapter, what scriptures or insights from S-FACTOR reveal that God doesn't want you to judge, but to truly love everyone?

"Judge not, that you be not judged. For with what judgment you judge, you will be judged; and with the measure you use, it will be measured back to you."
Matthew 7:1, 2

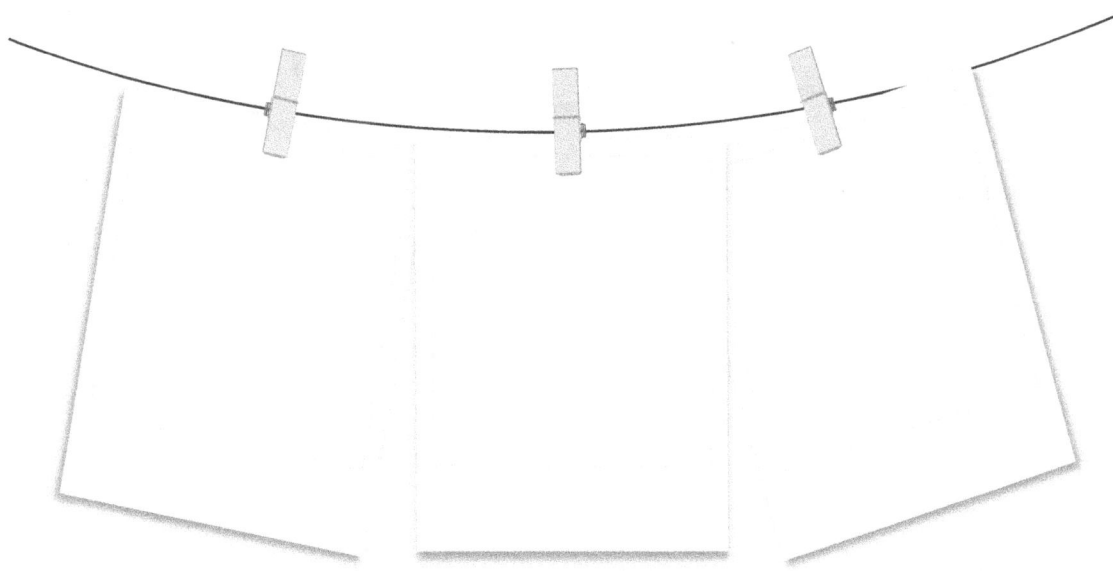

#SFactorPrayerJournal #PSML

S-Factor Prayer Journal

MY LIFE

Look in the mirror, what questions do you have? Can you accept your perfect imperfections and remind others they are wonderfully made?

QUESTIONS FOR GOD
DATE ASKED:

ANSWERS FROM GOD
DATE RECEIVED:

THESE FLAWS WON'T DEFINE ME

I'LL **COMPLIMENT SOMEONE** EACH DAY

S-Factor Prayer Journal

S-Factor Prayer Journal

PRAYER

> Do you realize that the Spirit is moving in your current circumstance? Pray for God to give you discernment, hindsight and foresight.

S-Factor Prayer Journal

If you prefer, you can express your PRAYER in a picture or drawing.

SAVED

Based on this chapter, what scriptures or insights from S-FACTOR have enlightened your awareness of the Spirit's role in your salvation?

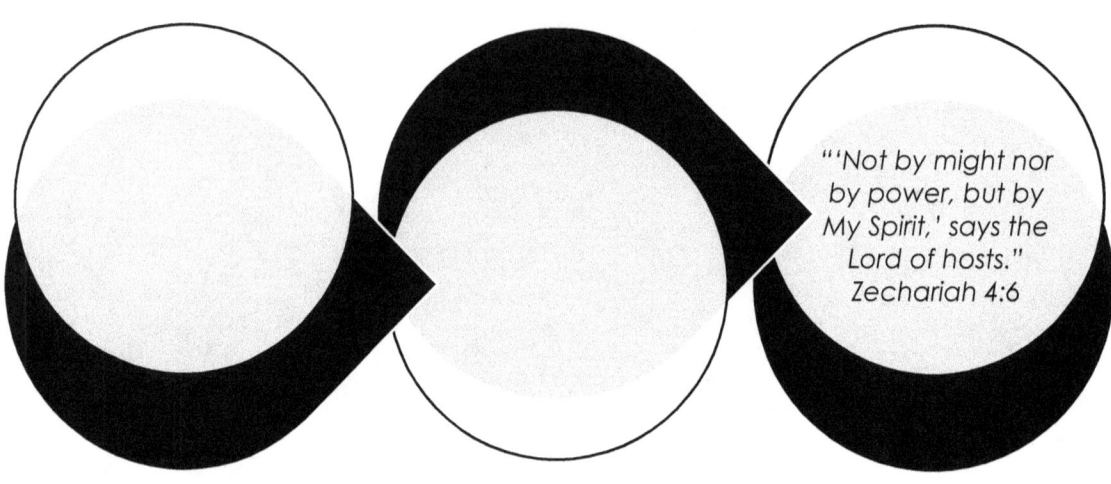

"'Not by might nor by power, but by My Spirit,' says the Lord of hosts."
Zechariah 4:6

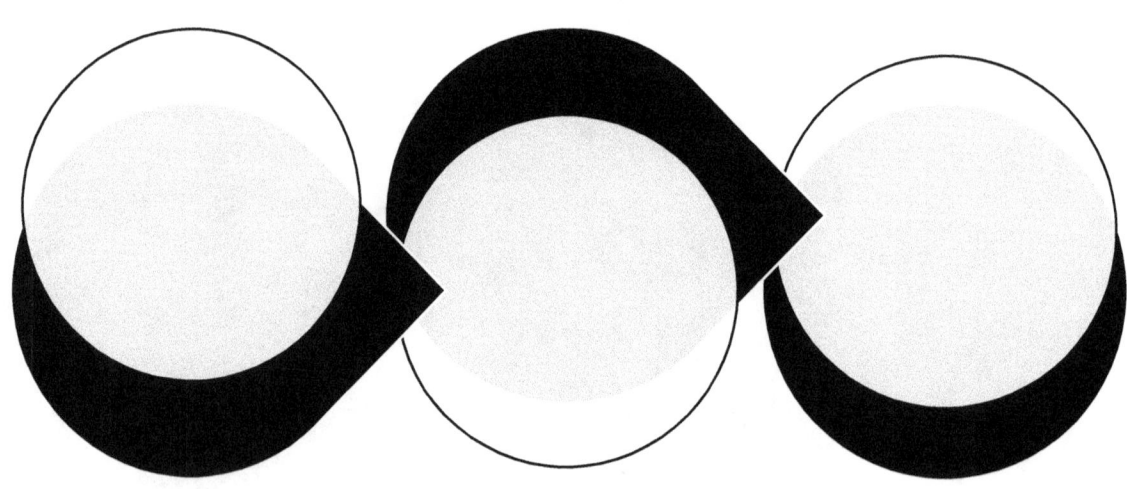

S-Factor Prayer Journal

MY LIFE

The Spirit is always moving. What questions do you have? When has the Spirit stirred up your situation? Did your blessings overflow to others?

QUESTIONS FOR GOD
DATE ASKED:

ANSWERS FROM GOD
DATE RECEIVED:

I'VE SEEN **THE SPIRIT MOVE** WHEN...

I'LL TELL OTHERS OF THE SPIRIT'S POWER

S-Factor Prayer Journal

S-Factor Prayer Journal

PRAYER

God speaks in many ways— the wind, earthquake, fire, or a still small voice. Pray that your ears and heart will always hear Him.

S-Factor Prayer Journal

If you prefer, you can express your PRAYER in a picture or drawing.

#SFactorPrayerJournal   #PSML

S-Factor Prayer Journal

SAVED

Based on this chapter, what scriptures or insights from S-FACTOR highlight the healing and transforming power of God's Word?

"Out of heaven He let you hear His voice, that He might instruct you; on earth He showed you His great fire, and you heard His words out of the midst of the fire."
Deuteronomy 4:36

#SFactorPrayerJournal   #PSML

S-Factor Prayer Journal

MY LIFE

Stop and listen—God is speaking to you. What questions do you have? Do you understand His message and are you sharing it?

QUESTIONS FOR GOD
DATE ASKED:

ANSWERS FROM GOD
DATE RECEIVED:

I'M LISTENING AND WILL OBEY

I'LL SHARE **GOD'S WORD** WITH…

#SFactorPrayerJournal   #PSML

S-Factor Prayer Journal

S-Factor Prayer Journal

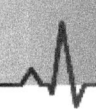

PRAYER

> We are all sinners saved by God's grace. Pray for those who don't know Jesus or who once accepted Him, but are now doubting.

S-Factor Prayer Journal

If you prefer, you can express your PRAYER in a picture or drawing.

S-Factor Prayer Journal

SAVED

Based on this chapter, what scriptures or insights from S-FACTOR give you the courage needed to help lead someone to Jesus.

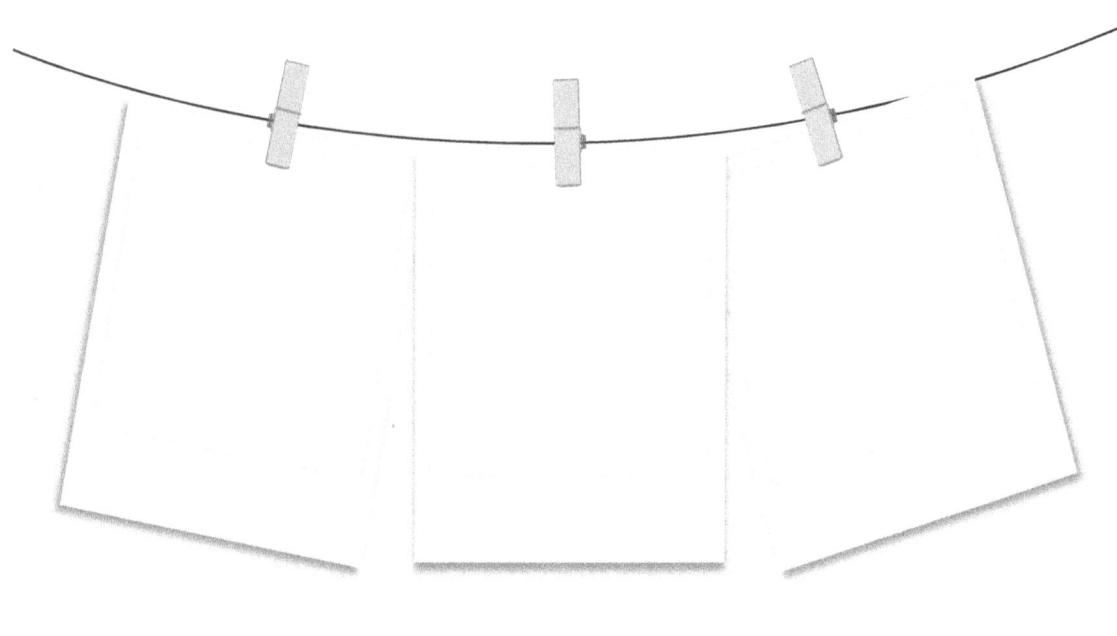

"How think ye? If a man have a hundred sheep, and one of them be gone astray, doth he not leave the ninety and nine, and goeth into the mountains, and seeketh that which is gone astray?"
Matthew 18:12, KJV

#SFactorPrayerJournal   #PSML

S-Factor Prayer Journal

MY LIFE

We fall down spiritually, but love picks us up. What questions do you have? Who helps you when you stumble and who can you pull up?

QUESTIONS FOR GOD
DATE ASKED:

ANSWERS FROM GOD
DATE RECEIVED:

I CAN OFTEN **RELY ON**

I CAN **STRENGTHENED** THOSE LOSING FAITH

#SFactorPrayerJournal

#PSML

S-Factor Prayer Journal

S-Factor Prayer Journal

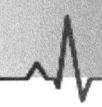

PRAYER

Many reject God's Word although they know it has the power to save. Pray for shackles to be broken and for captives to be set free.

S-Factor Prayer Journal

**If you prefer, you can express your PRAYER
in a picture or drawing.**

S-Factor Prayer Journal

SAVED

Based on this chapter, what scriptures or insights from S-FACTOR solidify that you can't be sincerely saved until you accept the gift of salvation?

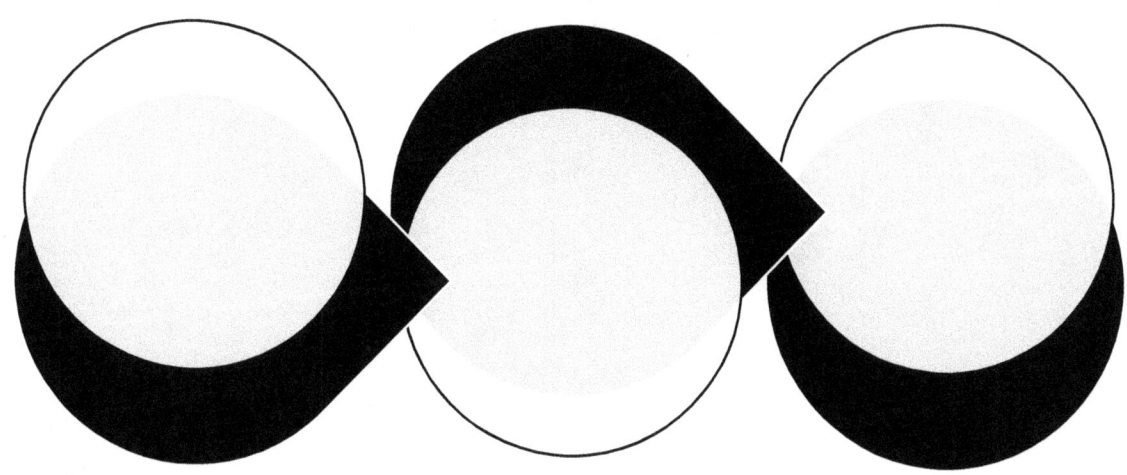

"Let the redeemed of the Lord say so, whom He has redeemed from the hand of the enemy."
Psalm 107:2

#SFactorPrayerJournal #PSML

S-Factor Prayer Journal

MY LIFE

> Remember, God had to intervene to save you. What questions do you have? How do you show gratitude and share your testimony?

QUESTIONS FOR GOD
DATE ASKED:

ANSWERS FROM GOD
DATE RECEIVED:

I'M **GRATEFUL** FOR THE GIFT OF SALVATION

I'LL **TELL MY STORY** TO OTHERS MORE OFTEN

#SFactorPrayerJournal #PSML

S-Factor Prayer Journal

S-Factor Prayer Journal

PRAYER

Sychar was about segregation and scandals until Jesus arrived in town. Fast and pray that sexism, racism, and all 'isms' will soon be destroyed.

S-Factor Prayer Journal

**If you prefer, you can express your PRAYER
in a picture or drawing.**

S-Factor Prayer Journal

SAVED

Based on this chapter, what scriptures or insights from S-FACTOR have motivated you to fast and pray for those thirsting for "living water?"

> "Therefore also now, saith the Lord, turn ye even to me with all your heart, and with fasting, and with weeping, and with mourning"
> Joel 2:12, KJV

#SFactorPrayerJournal #PSML

S-Factor Prayer Journal

MY LIFE

Sacrifice precedes salvation. What are your questions? Have you had a Sychar experience? What will you give up to lead others to Jesus?

QUESTIONS FOR GOD
DATE ASKED:

ANSWERS FROM GOD
DATE RECEIVED:

I WAS **TRANSFORMED** WHEN I MET JESUS HERE

I'LL SACRIFICE THIS TO **HELP SAVE** SOMEONE

#SFactorPrayerJournal   #PSML

S-Factor Prayer Journal

PRAYER

The question of "What If" should make you consider the ramifications of every choice and action. Pray earnestly before making each decision.

S-Factor Prayer Journal

**If you prefer, you can express your PRAYER
in a picture or drawing.**

SAVED

> Based on this chapter, what scriptures or insights from S-FACTOR make you appreciate that Jesus never wavered after pondering "What If?"

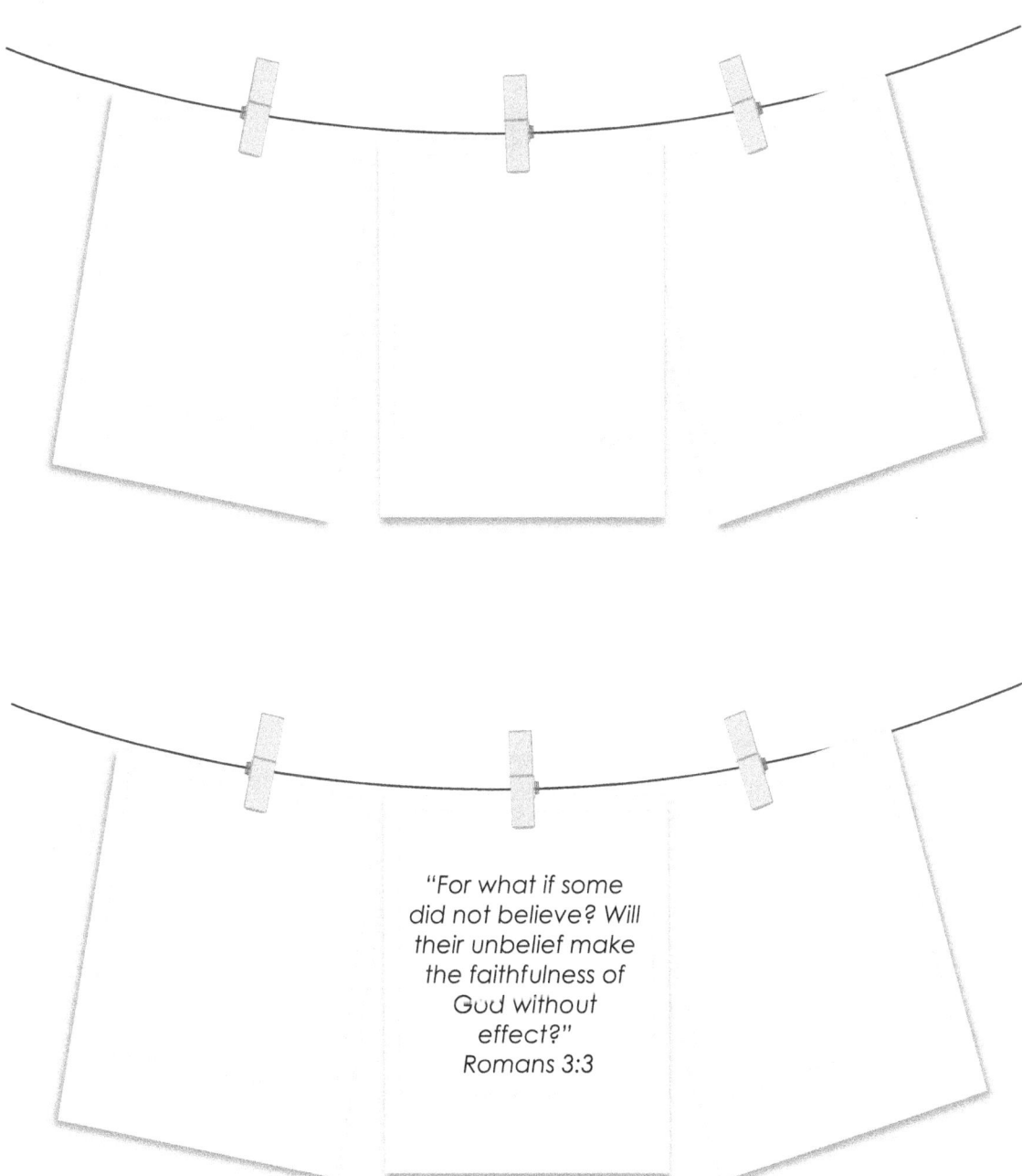

"For what if some did not believe? Will their unbelief make the faithfulness of God without effect?"
Romans 3:3

S-Factor Prayer Journal

MY LIFE

What if, Jesus refused to sacrifice Himself for our sins at Calvary? What questions do you have? What hope would there be for humanity?

QUESTIONS FOR GOD
DATE ASKED:

ANSWERS FROM GOD
DATE RECEIVED:

THESE **WHAT IFs** HAVE ME SEEKING GOD

I'LL **SERVE OTHERS** WITH A CHRIST-LIKE HEART

#SFactorPrayerJournal   #PSML

S-FACTOR highlights that Salvation Is...

FREE

I've intentionally mentioned it several times throughout SFACTOR. God crafted the plan of salvation before the existence of mankind. Jesus didn't ask us for anything before He voluntarily gave up His life on the cross at Calvary. We did not have to surrender anything or suffer on a cross. No matter what some theologians or religious leaders may want us to believe, **salvation is a free gift.**

HARDWORK

Just to be clear, we don't have to work for God to save us. He does it willingly, but once we accept His gift, we must unwrap it and begin to work. This work involves a lot of self-examination and daily surrendering of our desires and dreams to God's will. **This work is not easy, but it is absolutely necessary.**

JOURNEY

Each of us must decide whether or not we accept that "Christ is the Way, the Truth and the Life." Once we believe, the adventure begins. Sometimes our journey is filled with roses, but more often than not, it's overladen with thorns. **Regardless of the path**, we can't pack our s-factors—sins and sinful desires that separate us from God—and take them on this trip.

SWEET

Without a doubt, each of us should be able to say, "I have tasted and seen that the Lord is good" (Psalm 34:8). We shouldn't only serve God because of **how sweet salvation is** or because of the things He has done for us. We should serve Him because He is worthy. He is the Creator. He is the Alpha and Omega. He is the Everlasting Father. Who is Jesus to you?

S-Factor Prayer Journal

Salvation Is...

Fill in the blank based on your encounters with God.

The End

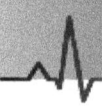
S-Factor Prayer Journal

If this journal has been helpful to you, we would love to hear what God has done in your life. Send your story to the Prayer Saved My Life team:

- www.prayersavedmylife.com (website)
- prayersavedmylife@gmail.com (email)

Please contact us if you have questions and/or want to learn more about joining our ministry and making a difference.

You can also show your support by following us on social media (use hashtags **#SFactorPrayerJournal**, **#SFactor**, and **#PSML**)

- Facebook.com/prayersavedmylife
- Instagram.com/prayersavedmylife
- Twitter.com/prayersavedmy

About the Author

Bridgette Bastien is a prayer enthusiast and the author of the *Prayer Saved My Life* Series. Writing a book was never on her bucket list until she was snatched from the jaws of death. After going through that experience, she had a reignited, burning desire to share the transformational power of prayer and to share the saving grace of God with others. She feasts on the Bible and, according to her daughters, "has playdates with her prayer group three times per day."

Bastien has written two books, OVERCOMER and S-FACTOR, and she has published several children's books written by her daughters. She was a research chemist early in her career, holds a master's degree in Strategy and Marketing from the Wharton School of Business—University of Pennsylvania, and is now a Marketing Professional. Bastien lives in Massachusetts with her family. She loves traveling the world, eating spicy foods, and basking in the warmth of her family and friends' love.

S-Factor Prayer Journal

Grateful for the Writing with Purpose Group:

Fiona Harewood is a published author of several books and a motivational speaker. Her book—*I Did It, You Can, Too!* is part of the Philadelphia School District's summer reading list. Harewood has a master's degree in public policy from Drexel University and works with the federal government. She lives in Philadelphia with her family and is a member of Mizpah SDA Church.

Harewood has a passion for writing, working with children, and using her gifts to glorify God. She often reflects on Proverbs 31:30, which says, *"Charm is deceitful and beauty is passing, but a woman who fears the Lord, she shall be praised.* Harewood says, "Salvation is what a wonderful Savior gave me when He hung on Calvary!"

Nathan Stephens is an innovative professional who delivers a comprehensive portfolio of services and results-oriented solutions designed to help align people, processes, and technology. With 20+ years of experience in professional IT service delivery, Nathan works closely with CIOs and IT Executives in various organizations. He is a customer advocate throughout all aspects of the customer lifecycle supported by Lean Six Sigma methodologies.

As a member of the Writing with Purpose Group, Nathan has been critical to the completion and publication of this prayer journal. He lives in the United Arab Emirates with his wonderful wife and is currently writing his first book. Stephens says, "Salvation is an everlasting peace. Even though I may sin, I will be saved by the grace of God."

S-Factor Prayer Journal

Prayer Can **SAVE** Your Life

S-Factor Prayer Journal

Special Edition
Resource Page

Dealing with Adversity

- OVERCOMER - Prayer Saved My Life Series by Bridgette Bastien (www.prayersavedmylife.com/books or www.amazon.com/dp/1732879818)
- RIVER NEVER SMOOTH by Fiona Harewood (www.amazon.com/dp/1647460522)

Suicide Prevention

- National Suicide Prevention Lifeline: (800) 273-8255; Available 24 hours

Depression and Mental Health

- Substance Abuse & Mental Health Services Administration: (800) 662-HELP (4357)

Bereavement and Compassionate Support

- Parents enduring the loss of a child: Compassionate Friends (630) 990-0010 (www.compassionatefriends.org)
- Directory of Grief Support Resources: My Grief Angels (www.mygriefangels.org)

Prayer and Building your Faith

- Prayer Saved My Life website (www.prayersavedmylife.com)
- Prayerline: (605) 313-5107 Code: 531755#; 5:00AM & 6:00PM EST (Sunday - Friday)

Learning more about Salvation

- *"Salvation in Symbols & Signs"* - A powerful series on the books of Daniel and Revelation hosted by James Rafferty and Ivor Myers (on YouTube)
- Study Guides available at https://salvationsymbols.tv/study-guides

www.ingramcontent.com/pod-product-compliance
Lightning Source LLC
Chambersburg PA
CBHW081326040426
42453CB00013B/2311